The Cunning Person's
Poetry Apothecary

Written and Illustrated by
Maryam Elen Jones

Chthonia Books

Introduction

This book is born out of my fascination with the hidden world of the cunning folk, who were marginalised people, attempting in some way to gift medicine, and with it power, to disempowered people. If you can identify with aspects of this description, this book is for you.

In writing this book, I drew on my own life, and my own cunning. I have attempted to share that cunning, both magical and practical, distilled into magical poems and initiatory images, each one designed to awaken some aspect of your cunning gifts.

I hope you will find this book medicinal. Use it how you will. I honour you. I honour your cunning.

Elen

Birth

Cunning folk were often skilled midwives, with a deep knowledge of the birth process in all its fullness.

Birth is a deep mystery, which cannot be understood by mind alone: the physiology of birth is one tiny aspect of something extraordinary.

Many things must be birthed, and to be present here is to be birthed, and to birth: every sentence we utter, every word we put to paper, each creative act we ever make, each caress, or action, is a kind of birth, a showing up to the process of existence.

From a cunning perspective, every birth is also a death, and a loss: the dark safety of the womb has to end when what is inside comes to form and light.

This is a poem about birth, to aid the birther, and the child.
Bear down, they say, right into the root.
Push, push, push. Harder.
But what if, I didn't?
What if I stopped trying, to birth at all?
What if what was to birth sang, like a red river, through my
soul, and spoke, like this:
Stop, Trying. Stop, Trying.
Oh God, is it worth it, at all?
To put out life, when I must break that beautiful darkness,
Where all is held?
Where all is songed, and free.
Does God birth, like a strange little woman?
Or like some sweat-soaked thing, bearing down.
Sweating, intense, undrugged, and wild?
I was born, for this.
To be it all: babe, and birthing one, and midwife.
I cannot stop, that's the truth, however harsh the doctors.
My whole life, like a wild song, to the hidden courage, of
birthing.

Oppression

To be oppressed is to discover cunning, in all its senses. One of the most bitter aspects of oppression is that it is often a hidden pain: there becomes no language to convey to others what is occurring, and isolation sets in.

Our natural responses to oppression have been crushed: anger is choked, defiance is unseen, and guilt can be a constant companion.

There is no answer to oppression that is logical or linear. We have to go deep into the roots of things, and uncover what is rotten.

To be cunning is to survive against the odds, not to be crushed, entirely, and to refuse to give up the 'taste' of who you are, even if it disgusts or challenges others.

The lowly, disregarded, contempted, have their own language. Sometimes all you can do, is spit in the butter, or shove a few herbs where the sun don't shine.

Against the odds, I live.

I, the soft field, where you plant insults, growing like wild barley.

I, walked on, like so much land.

Your acres, not my own.

I am your pasture, for you to sow wheat, and seeds of hate.

My children, are yours, do with them what you will.

I can't always be coming back.

Sometimes, I have to go, and let your shoes walk, on me, seemingly forever.

Still, I am land, filthy with your lies, utterly polluted, but land nonetheless.

Sometimes, the only choice, is to be spoiled land, or the land's owner, eternally walking his plot.

I made that choice, long ago.

I will never be the boot.

That I know.

I will never walk, on someone else's back.

As you do, farmer.

Facing Down Cult-Like Behaviour

Cunning is an ignition of your own 'nous', which is inherently resistant to rule-bound conformity.

Families, religious or spiritual groups, even workplaces can become suffused with cult-like functioning and the signs are hard to spot.

The mind can be easily bamboozled by gaslighting techniques, and even the heart can be confused, as in cult-like settings our own natural compassion is weaponised: 'why do you care about this, and then go and do that?' Dropping into the gut instinct can be hard, but anxiety, distress and confusion rarely lie.

Trust yourself, in all things, first. Sometimes you are the only guide you have. If you find yourself in situations where consulting your own wisdom has become taboo, it's natural to feel uneasy and afraid. But you deserve freedom.

I walked to the edge of your cult, and rested there.
Four trees came, each one anchored to my soul.
I'm not your anchoress, anymore, to be locked in a small cell,
with a brindled cat.
If you wanted me to stay walled in, why give me a cat?
Licking her brindled fur, my cat purred, and told me truths.
She discerned, what I could not: that all the world believes
your lies, except my own skin,
Which prickles.
You seem so generous, and so kind.
But my fur is bristling, and my back can't help but arch.
My cat is spitting, and pawing the door, where your feet once
were.
I haven't seen a leaf, for years.
But you let me have a cat.
I learn, when I am alone, from my cat's oddness, to be wise,
and wilder, every day.
And there, you made an error.

Emotional Surveillance

Human emotion has an essential protective function, helping us to know what is needed in any given situation. Many systems of control, including oppressive spiritual systems will seek to regulate emotion through constant surveillance and feed back: 'calm down, there's no need to get so emotional.'

One of the traditional roles of cunning folk was emotional display: keening or other public rituals designed to harness the emotional power of the land, and to make inner states public.

It is important to remember that emotional repression has its own cunning: we are so used to regulating our own emotional range and that of others, it becomes second nature from an early age. Even joy, play and natural enthusiasm are taboo in many social situations, almost from the start of our lives.

Never doubt that your emotional range matters: to you, to your kin, to the land.

Part-banshee am I.
The keening, just happens.
Hot lava coming, like good bread.
My anger, like a fire-sheet rises.
Wanting to cleanse the land, of what hate can do.
Sometimes, burning is like balm.
Blistering off, the false face, I learned at my mother's knee.
Father's hate, or sadness, is a sickness, in the land.
Like the fisher king's wound.
It festers.
I keen the God that is not afraid, of my face, when tears flow.
That wants me to find anger, when I see things burn.
My own nature, aligned so deeply in, that I know, just know,
when to rage, or keen, and when to fall quiet, and knit
blankets, or shrouds.
But I will not shroud, until I must, my own flame.
I will rekindle, secretly if I must, that flame.
For in my fire, some of the pain burns,
I clean this forest.

Emotional Exploitation

Emotional exploitation is how things work, often enough, in modern culture, and going back a long way.

We are told that this is a 'dog eat dog' world, but, in truth, dogs rarely eat dogs, so for us to 'go for' other human beings requires incredible emotional deadening. This is exhausting. And yet, we are often also faced with a paradoxical pressure to be infinitely compassionate, and not to have any boundaries on our love.

Spiritual systems can also be exhausting. Many practices involve conformity, and even ruthlessness, as spontaneous displays of individual emotion are usually frowned on. But paradoxically, we are also encouraged to be 'infinitely compassionate' with a 'boundless heart.'

Hearts are not boundless. Compassion is as precious and beautiful a natural resource as wood, coal, or oil. You cannot extract and extract compassion from a person, and expect them not to burn out.

I'm dog-tired, of your world.
My little heart, is all broken.
Sensitive, at heart, I can be ruthless, now.
I'm often cruel.
You made me thus, with your demands.
'Rub my knees,' you said, 'and now rub all the others, too.'
I'm exhausted, really tired, and I can't sleep,
So I crawl, on my knees, to the old statues.
Mother Mary, with a red heart, oozing love.
'How can I stay here,' I ask, 'and not die, of the heart-pain. I'm
so open.
My heart, is so bruised.'
'My dear one,' she says, 'you're not a bleeding saint.
You're not a statue.
Neither am I, though they paint me thus:
Simultaneously cold, and bleeding-open.
Icy, and bloody, both.'
She folds herself out of the cold wood,
And comes home, with me.
We rest, together.

Defeat

Living in a profoundly unjust society, defeat is a constant companion: if not our own, then that of those we see around us every day. In a 'winners and losers' world, there must be many losers for one person to win. We are encouraged to push this aside, or, even worse, to blame ourselves for our own losses.

The feeling of defeat is sometimes almost unbearable. We want to escape the feeling and push it aside, and yet, it persists.

The cunning folk were defeated, over and over again. Most of them were born with the odds stacked against them: no healthcare, no money, extreme poverty and injustice, racism, sexism.

They faced what we face, and their wisdom was defeated, by and large. Sometimes, you will not win, and cannot win. But you can persist, and recognise the courage that takes.

If you think you are beaten, you are, some say.
I got beat, and I know I'm beaten.
If you think you dare not, you don't.
I dare not say, you're wrong.
That years and years of ground-in pain, has scarred the earth.
And that the trees scream.
That the earth herself, is next-to-dead.
Your world, so tawdry.
And now, you tell me this, that it's in my head,
The winning, and losing.
My worth, is all the pain.
The pain, of all the ones, who will not win, cannot, ever.
I'm done. Just done.
I'll lay here, on the earth's belly,
And be, as I am.
Not even trying.
There is defiance, in that.
I will not win, the game,
But I will not die, either.

Corruption

Facing corruption is an old task for the cunning person. In the days before antibiotics and modern hygiene, it would be impossible to overlook the outward signs of bodily corruption.

From a cunning perspective, the healing of corruption is a slow process, involving exposure to light, sun, air, and plant medicine.

In our modern world, we are still much-troubled by corruption, but much of it is inner: the slow festering of wounds which were never ours to bear.

Corruption has its own strange beauty, and it is part of life: death, decay and dissolution are part of the natural world, and without them we would be in a very unhealthy place indeed.

It is cunning to have a deep respect for what is corrupt, knowing that it has its own timescales, language and relationship to the healthy whole.

I dreamed this: that I faced a pot, oozing with strange things.
Fungi, and thready worms, and black bile.
The ordinary filth, of my inner world.
It was not unpleasant, to face this pot, and dip my hand in,
and make magic.
Taking out the wiggling worms, that eat my soul.
Then a man came, with a smart car, and took a dim view, of all
my dipping in.
My child-like joy, at exploring the pot.
It released his own worms, and mine, crawling over the
smooth leather, of his drive.
If I stir my pot, and let out some of the contents, I will
contaminate his world, with knowledge.
His charms are many, and his car is fast.
But I never get to hold the map.
Today, I let the pot speak.
I didn't crawl, so low.
My back straightened.
The curve of my spine, my own.

Intimidation

Cunning folk often operated in secret, and in great terror of the church and court authorities, and there is no doubt that some cunning people used intimidation themselves in the form of curses and other threats to terrorise and silence their perceived foes.

But the very existence of cunning folk is a testimony to the power of intimidated people to develop their own knowledge, power and spiritual systems.

Becoming less intimidated is a cunning process, and often painfully slow. Nothing is more powerful than having access to your own inherent worth, which is precisely why any oppressive system will spend much time and energy on intimidation.

Timidity is a protective 'coat' which sometimes must be worn for a lifetime, but with cunning, you can choose where, when and how closely to wear it.

I am in love with any church, or temple, or any kind of shrine.
But rarely do they love me back.
So I have become timid.
Kept my ears back, and curled, my small tail under, when I felt alone.
Scuttled round the edge, of churches, like a rat.
Intimidated, by power, and smoothness of form.
Life, is mostly small, and often scruffy.
Snarled up, with the entangled web.
Not smooth, like churches.
But churches are few, and far between, compared to bugs, and rats and all that.
Compared to the crawling nature, of nature.
Compared to all the things, that ever had a heart, what's a church?
Just a place, where rats crawl, at night, in secret.
Where squirrels nest, and chew the roof, bare.
Much damage, can be done, you know, by small things, that crawl, low.
When you are not looking.

Despair

An old word for despair is wanhope. There is a specific pain in being without hope: we can no longer sustain the thread that keeps us trying, and struggling, to get through.

Sustaining hope in the face of overwhelming struggle is a task that requires much cunning. Sometimes we have to sink further in for hope to return organically. Despair can turn to desperation, leading to sudden action after all. What is there to lose?

In all honesty, I don't have an 'answer' or solution for despair, except perhaps to give it room to be present at the table.

Modern terms such as depression can mask old-fashioned problems like despair. The battle against despair is so old, that there must be some balm lurking in the land of 'what has been' against it. Perhaps it has its own voice that can speak to what needs confronting, honouring or letting be.

There is a woman, I know, called Wanhope.
She lives by me, day and night.
Her skirts rustle, with old charms.
I know her well, so well she is my love.
We have laid long years in the dry grass, and thought of
nothing but despair.
She makes nothing.
She has nothing.
She holds nothing, like a dry tongue, that whispers.
Sometimes, when I am low enough, and the world has won
again, she sings, and the voice is like threads.
And I plait despair, with the withies.
Then, I make baskets, with my own despair,
And no one can stop me.
I refuse the tablets, and the mind doctor's spells.
I refuse to be cheered on.
I remain, skirted with despair.
For I know she will ignite me, with hope, when the time is
right again.
For she is also flame, my old woman Wanhope.

Burden

Burden comes from the old root word byrthen, which means a load or weight, and also a child (as in birth). Sometimes, cunning itself is a burden.

Ignorance can be bliss, and the desire to help and heal others can leave us run ragged with others' problems. It is not always easy to know what is ours to bear, or how to bear it without breaking.

The practical, tangible, world can be intensely healing when we are overburdened: coming back to the root of life, where everything is joined.

Child-rearing is an old mystery of small steps: washing, dressing, feeding. Much of the energy of cunning people would have been spent on tending children, and helping them through ailments.

Knowing what ails you is a relief: confusion can become an intense burden, leading us to take on problems which were never ours. It is cunning to know what you can, and cannot do.

Burden is my name, and I bear much.
Warming the cold water, in the harsh dish.
Taking wands, and making circles, that bleed pain.
Arching my back, that is tired, and old.
Dancing, in a strong circle.
All this I do, burdened with unseeing eyes.
For I look in the mirror, and see not, the hundred burdens I
have eased, for other folk.
I look, and see more, more, more, that I never did.
All the babes, that go too soon, over.
I come to the old pot, in my own kitchen, and it is cold.
For I spent long hours making supper, for all the village.
Dolling out lumps, of clay, and blood, and chalk.
Writing messages, on sand.
Easing burdens.
The pot is cold, but I have fire, within.
Enough to light a match, and put the pot on, again, to bubble.
Burden is my name, and I will get my own dinner.

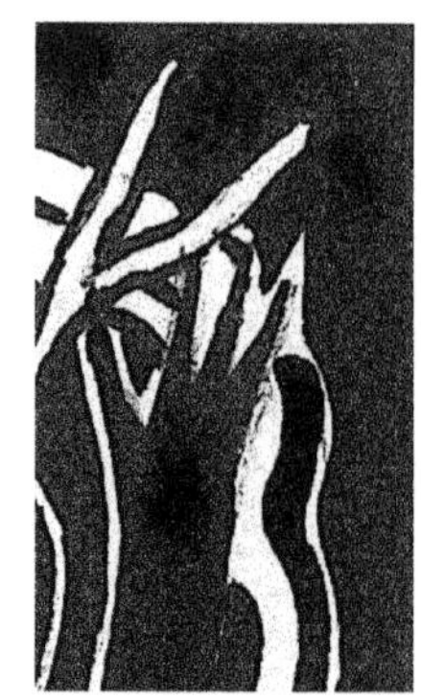

Dryness

Thirst is one of the most primal human sensations. Our relationship with water is so close that we need to take it physically into our bodies many times a day.

We are embodied water, and yet water remains a mystery to us. Our culture can be very 'dry' and cerebral, with little attention given to the 'wetness' of imagination, sensuality and magic. More and more children are being asked to 'swim on dry land,' which gets exhausting.

The cunning folk may well have used water in healing spells, and had special relationships with wells, springs, and rivers. Knowing how to reconcile the wet and dry in the patient would have been an important focus for healing.

You cannot ever be a dry thing, no matter how thirsty you feel. You are here to wet the dry land, and there is that within you which can never run dry.

I leafed through an old book, dry as a bone.
Written by seven men, who scraped the words on the page,
with pens that soon ran dry.
Even the ink despaired, of what they wrote.
Their words were dry, parched, and dusty.
Leaves need the wet.
Pages need the dew, the rain, the vast sea, of a wild song,
pounding on the paper.
I cannot scrape by, anymore, on others' words.
My mermaid tail is growing.
Daring to be wet, when all the land is parched, is no doubt
risky.
I could get sold, in a big cage, and married to a dry husband,
who gives me two legs, of sand.
I could get put on a pew, in the fine church, and lose my mind,
hiding.
But I am so dry, I must risk it all, diving deep.
Over, and over, into my own waters.
Coming up wet, and salty.

Unsounded

We were born to make sounds. From the first, we are sounded creatures: screaming for attention, help, love.

Sadly, our culture or our family systems can be deaf to our soundings, and we can slowly learn that to be 'good' is to be silent, or at least selectively silent: to speak only about what is acceptable, 'nice' and safe.

The cunning folk recognised the power of sound. Spells, songs and even curses give voice to what ails us, what inspires us, what we dread, what we know.

There is a familial lineage between shamanism and cunning practices, and every shaman knows the power of intuitive sound, born in the moment, from what must speak.

It is dangerous, and even reckless to leave sound to fester in the land, whether the human land of our bodies, or the wider land of our world.

Unsounded, am I.
Just a slow rhythm, of words, on paper.
Tap, tap, tap.
The sound of a crow, high in my own tree, squawking.
Caw, caw, caw!
He was never silenced, that crow.
He gave me six feathers, to make music come, in my own soul.
His voice, is like every poetry, that ever was, to me
Caw! Caw! Caw!
I can't even begin, to make a sound, as sweet as what he
makes.
But I am sounded, with words, and language.
Whole languages of mine are now dead.
What's that? You want me silent?
Plenty of time, for that, when I am dead.
Then, and only then, will I be compliant.
Or maybe not even then.
For death is not the worst, and not the end, of sound.
Caw! Caw! Caw!
You see, I am still sounded.

29

Broken

We live in a culture that aggressively values the new over the old, the whole over the broken.

There is a certain magic in what is old, broken, or wounded. Many old stories tell of a young man who must marry or kiss a hideous old woman, in order to release a young princess within.

The magic of the old hag is timeless, and rich: it is the magic of what has fully lived, and been scarred, broken, changed, in the process.

Cunning folk would almost certainly have some age to them: cunning is something built and refined over a lifetime.

Whatever age you are, if you are old enough to read and understand this, you will have been broken in some way. Rather than seek to make yourself whole again, as you were before, is there some way in which you can harness the power of breakage?

This is a song, to broken things.
Come out, come out.
Be seen, and known, for what you are.
Yes, you are broken.
But you are not a china doll, that cracks in shards, and is
suddenly ruined, smashing on the cold floor.
You are not a doll, simpering and sweet, always perfect.
Some calming thing, given to fools to hold, so they can
become bolder, in your breaking.
Oh no. If you are a doll, you are like the ones made by old
witches.
Bound, with black thread, round and round. Herbal, inside.
Soaked, with what you know.
You have a choice, my dear.
To stay as broken dolly, with a china face, that the world likes,
well enough,
Or to be like a ragged thing, that no one wants, but you.
A talisman, of power, and strange feelings.
Made by old hands.
Ragged, with a herbal centre.

31

Unbirded

Many cunning folk kept the faery faith, which held that all things have voice, language, enchantment.

Even though we now know and by and large accept the facts of evolution, we are yet to re-absorb the 'heart' of this truth: that it is highly unlikely that we are 'above' the other animals, and that we share many of the same traits, impulses, and gifts with them.

To re-absorb this knowledge now, not just with our minds, but with our bodies, is a pressing task, for the arrogance, greed, shame and dissociation birthed from the old teachings is literally destroying our world. Without our allies in the animal and plant kingdoms, we become small, lonely and isolated.

Cunning folk who could communicate in any way with animals were seen as wicked witches communing with 'familiars.' But our very lives depend on becoming familiar again with the animal world, and our own animality.

When did you become, unbirded?
Once, you soared, as birds do, higher and higher, with a wild sky listening.
You flew. You really did.
That day, those days, you were winged, and you were bird.
You think I lie.
That you were never feathered.
If there is a God, it is inside you, and me.
Inside each egg, and beak, and bird, and feather.
What does such a God want, from its kin?
Just to peck, peck, peck, at each other, in a dry barn, till they are dead?
To be the farmer, of such a barn, where the hand hates the foot, for being feathered?
Or to be at one, with the one you are.
To make good things, with the hands you have.
To grow a type of wings, a sort of song, while you are not too old.
To become as you are. Birded.

Prey

Predator-prey behaviour is deeply rooted in animal life. This truth is problematic to many spiritual systems, and the emphasis is often on 'escaping' the predator/prey cycle, by 'ascending' into our 'true nature.'

There will always be predators, but systematic abuse is perhaps uniquely human.

All the many hours we have spent in meditation and silent prayer have not made us universally kind and good. Those who have moved in spiritual circles for long enough know that even kindness and goodness can become weapons in the right hands, and the most benign women's circle can descend into a bloodbath.

It is cunning to know that such behaviour is an inherent part of who we are, linking us deeply to the rhythms, concerns, and wisdom of our allies: the many, many past selves who lived here, and knew how to get food by predation, or stay alive by escaping predators.

This is a poem, to all the prey.
For every mouse, eared with tension.
Oh, how can I keep that sweetness, which is my heart, and not get punched, and kicked, and bit?
How can I live, a long life, and not get strangled?
Your own sweetness, is like sugar, that runs. Like honey.
But honey is guarded by bees. It never sits alone, just waiting to be had.
So much, is bitter, now.
The many, many, who have no sweetness left at all, rampage about, making havoc.
To such a one, you will always be prey.
Then, you must find your bee.
Sting, sting, sting again, if you have to.
Just enough, to guard that honey.
For the world needs that.
It is so sour here, that sweetness is medicine, to every soul.
And thieves assault the hive, at every turn.
Bite back, and guard the honey.

Unmothered

We are living in a world that is profoundly unmothered. With the coming of patriarchal religions, and possibly even before that, we have spiralled into a time where the father principle rules supreme, and profoundly distorted.

Finding the places within you that have been unmothered is a thankless and heartbreaking task. It can lead to an increase in the feelings of brokenness.The process of becoming consciously unmothered is excruciating, but nowhere near as harmful as the state of being unconsciously unmothered, which is where we have been forced to dwell.

The position of cunning people and their status reveals both a profound need for wise mothering, in all its forms, and also how contempted such an energy really is in a patriarchal, militaristic world.

Do not give up. To take small steps towards the unmothered within you, is a mothering action.

This is a poem, for the unmothered.
Did you lose the way, little one, and get lost?
Many's the time, we all wished, to be mothered.
Motherless, we go on.
No mothers, anymore.
No fathers, either.
Just a father god, with a bald face, and blank pews.
Stained, with sorrows.
Mother, is there a face that sits, in the pew, that looks like
you?
That has some tinge, about it, of what is tender?
That has some time, to sit, and be still, with the lost heart, of a
world with no mothers.
For this is an unsuckled time.
A time, of sad children, with axes, then stones, then swords,
then gunfire.
A time of the dead tree, and the broken pitcher.
A time of no knitting, no sewing, nothing well-mended.
No dad to mend the nets, that cutting broke.
Nothing about, but the songs, that speak, of dead mothers.

Disorder

Disorder is one of the building blocks of life. The constant interplay of chaos and order is observable throughout the natural world. Out of this dance, structure and life emerges. Yet we live in cultures which highly value conformity and often equate this with order.

Cunning folk were, by and large, those who could not or would not conform to the social structures of their time. To be cunning is to have constant communion with the strange, the ill, the outcasted, and to let it speak.

The disordered self can be likened to a 'happy outcast' - that strange woman at the edge of the village who has little to lose and therefore is unimpressed by pretty prizes. But outcast her too far, and she can become truly destructive.

Can you allow what is disordered, deranged, unstable, intensely creative within you to speak, without judging yourself to be mad, bad, or defective?

This is a poem, of disorder.
Behind this world is order.
But not as you know:
Not rigid, fixed, like ruled lines, or old-book-men.
Order, breeds in my mind, with her dark sister chaos.
Two sisters, who make babies come.
Worlds, stars, planets, swans.
IT junkies, kids, stones.
All of it, a sacred child, of order, and disorder.
Some say my mind's too fast, or slow.
That I am rigid, stupid, or retarded.
Selfish, or diseased.
But I am merely this:
A magic child, spun from a silken thread.
A wild song, of my two mothers.
I am half mad, like all the rest.
Frogs, fish, jam, wanking.
What kind of God made those?
A wild one, just like me.
A gorgeous boy, born of two wilful mothers.

Gaslit

Gaslighting is a modern term, for an old phenomenon, which would have been familiar to the cunning folk.

Intuition, magical thinking, deep relationships with animals, dream-walking and trance work, are deeply embedded in who we are, and our oldest spiritual practices reflect this.

In the old film Gaslight, the perpetrating husband uses a range of trickery to convince the wife her perceptions are insane, including dimming the gaslight in their home, and denying he has done so.

When we discount all our old gifts and ways, we dim the world, and dim our perceptions. This matters even more when we are being bullied, oppressed or manipulated, as the conscious mind is only a fraction of our 'thinking self.' Often, it is only the subliminal self that has any sense of who we truly are, and what is happening to us. Fearful as it is to use this buried 'light' it is sometimes the only way we can escape from the dark.

Gaslit, am I.
Said to be broken.
The man who hovers on the stair, is greedy.
He wants it all: the whole body, the whole house, and all the world.
Should I trust such a man, who tells me my richness is a kind of squalor?
His heart is rotten to the core, whisper the strange voices, round my bed,
Is he my good knight, or my infernal devil?
The old house creaks.
I creep out suddenly, to seek allies.
In the street outside, the streetlamps whisper, 'you are mad, quite mad, now.'
Perhaps I am.
But in the madness of the street, I am tasting freedom.
I'll sit till dawn, there.
Watching the morning sun come up, like an old friend.
While my broken self is tucked up still in bed, with a hot drink, dozing.

Grooming

Grooming is subtle, and hard to distinguish from genuine connection.

At last, the sickening realisation happens that we were being groomed all along, and suddenly we are left bereft, and alone, trying to piece together the stolen parts of ourselves. But when our genuine desire for love, approval, and connection have been used to ensnare us, somehow our very innocence itself seems tainted and distrustful. We learn to distrust our natural sweetness.

I cannot say in all honesty that I have any words to pour balm on this one, except to say I speak as a victim of grooming myself. The way back is slow, painful and scarred. But know that you were not at fault, in any way, if you have been groomed. Your sweetness can never truly be stolen. It is yours, and remains yours, even if the road back seems unbearably slow.

I was groomed.
Gently betrayed, little-by-little.
To be betrayed, for all you are, is harsh.
Taken in, little-by-little.
Until you reach the house, of gingerbread steps.
Even then, it looks nice, sweet, normal.
There are no signs.
The door barely creaks.
The windows look wise, and glossy.
All the charms, are there.
And sat inside, who could be nicer?
Click, clack, and again, I'm in the oven.
Know this: your innocence did not come here empty-handed,
to be shut, again and again, in ovens.
You have allies.
The very earth, cries out, against such harms.
For innocence, is gold, and it is silver.
Unharmed, by any act, and utterly harmed, that's true.
Come in, my dear child, come deeper in, and find the secret
door, in the oven's back, that leads to a deep forest.

Deforested

We are forest-born creatures, living by and large away from our old home. The cunning folk kept alive a connection with forested places, and perhaps some of them slept or lived in the woods, out of necessity. Their awareness of tree lore, plant medicine and the forested self was seen as dangerous and 'dark' by those who persecuted them. For so long, our conception of the divine has been bound up with human light, outcasting the dark woods to scary stories. Our only remaining vestige of tree lore is a sterile cross.

To become re-forested is frightening, isolating, awful. Walking back into the woods is not a light-hearted adventure, but a quest for what is truly dark, and what has been placed in the dark by our own consciousness. The forest never leaves us, even if we burn it down or cut it out a hundred times.

I was deforested, long ago.
Taken, against my will, out of the dark forest.
Strapped to a cart, and seeing the trees go away.
Maybe I walked, a proud young thing, out of the forest.
Perhaps I packed a hamper, of all things good.
Fully intending, to come back later.
Kissing the brown surface of each tree, and saying goodbye.
My tears, wetting the wood.
I came back, with a big axe, years later, and cut it all down.
The stupid forest.
I felled each tree.
Now, years later, I come again, to the dry patch, where the trees once stood.
There, in the barren floor, is a secret doorway.
A place of terror, that's for sure, but rich with stories, words, pictures.
I can't hide from that.
In the end, I must come back, to what is lost.
In the end, I must come back, and bury the hatchet.

Distraction

It is difficult sometimes to know what distraction is. The literal meaning of the word is 'to turn away from a point,' which seems simple enough, but what is the 'point' we should be focusing on?

At school, or in work, we are used to being scolded when we are distracted from some mundane and unpleasant task, but often this is just healthy adaptation to overload or boredom.

Spiritual systems often give us points of focus, but these can become restrictive and boring.

No one else can define for you what the 'point' is. Not this book, any cunning person, alive or dead, not any news organisation, church, political party, friend, lover, parent.

Your own cunning knows what is the 'point' just now. Maybe it is catching up with Facebook, or zoning out with a comforting movie. Nothing is more 'spiritual' than nourishing your own soul.

I have been distracted, yes.
I eat, from the common trough, of lies.
I can't feel what a dog can feel, under his four paws.
I could learn a lot, from any pig.
I can try, to be like him,
Putting my snuffling nose, to the earth, and taking sips.
Smelling the black earth, and what it is saying.
Listening, with a snouted nose, to the four paws, of my
mother.
Maybe she whispers, through screens.
Perhaps she talks, in the dry words of politicians.
But I know this: she cares, and so do I.
That's why I need so much distraction.
For the black earth sings a sad song, often enough, of many
woes.
Whitened, as she is, with exploitation.
What should be black, and moist, is white, thin, and dry,
almost like ashes.
What should be black, and moist, is white, and thin, and dry,
almost like ashes.

47

Marginalised

Mainly, cunning people lived outside the literate world. They lived marginalised at best, but mostly 'beyond the book', living and dying without written trace, unless they came into conflict with the law. Their own lore was passed on mouth to mouth.

Books and words matter. We learn early in life who or what deserves to be on the page. Often, it is too terrifying to make a mark, for we are sure to be punished, even by our own terror of ruining the narrative for others.

'Beyond the book' people have a choice: to make our mark, or live and die in silence. Taking up the pen or pencil is a heavy burden. Perhaps without doing so you are able to fit very well into someone else's story, and gain the rewards of that. But the margins matter. Sometimes they are the only place that we can write at all.

I am on the margins.
I lie. I vanished.
Isn't it nicer, without my scrawl, on the white page?
I can't write neatly.
When I pick up my pen, it's all loops, and doodles. Ugly.
The page without me tells a good tale.
I am poor, and that's not good.
Rich in courage, to think about coming back.
For I know what happens, when I stain the page.
Blotting the copybook, I kept so nicely.
Copying the old words, of a thousand men, who know so much.
Making straight lines, and endless pointless patterns, to conform.
I will die, if I do not make my mark.
But if I do, I will be on the first cart, out of this village.
I can smell the wood from here, and the fire, they have made.
My life will be destroyed, but the mark will stay.
That's the choice, you know, often enough, if you live on the margins.

*An apothecary of enchantments to activate
your cunning...*

The cunning folk were marginalised people, attempting in some way to gift medicine, and with it power, to disempowered people. Little is known of their lives, but their wisdom lives on in the ancestral memory.

Much of our education, even spiritual education, is concerned with making us 'people of the book,' following the guidance of others who have come before, and written down their wisdom. There is nothing wrong with this approach, it has taken us far, and given us many gifts, but it is not the whole story...

9 7 9 8 3 3 0 2 7 2 4 0 2